Our Lives, Our World

Denmark

South Huntington Pub. Lib.
145 Pidgeon Hill Rd.
Huntington Sta., N.Y. 11746

Chrysalis Education

This US edition copyright © 2006 Chrysalis Education
Published in conjunction with Chrysalis Books Group Plc

Copyright © Chrysalis Books Group Plc 2005
Photography © Kristian Buus, Lene Esthave
and Toke Hage 2005

International copyright reserved in all countries.
No part of this book may be reproduced in any form
without written permission from the publisher.

Distributed in the United States by
Smart Apple Media
2140 Howard Drive West
North Mankato, Minnesota 56003

Library of Congress Control Number: 2004108808

ISBN 1-59389-228-4

Compiled and edited by Susie Brooks
Associate Publisher: Joyce Bentley
Designed by: Tall Tree Books Ltd
Photographic consultant: Jenny Matthews
Photographic coordinator: Kristian Buus
Picture researcher: Miguel Lamas
Translator: Kristian Buus

Printed in China

10 9 8 7 6 5 4 3 2 1

The Publishers would like to thank the photographers,
Kristian Buus, Lene Esthave, and Toke Hage, for
capturing these wonderful children on film. Many thanks
also to Kristian for his support and encouragement
throughout the project.

Corbis: Ray Juno 4(BR), Bob Krist 5(CL); Courtesy of Danmarks
Nationalbank 22(BL); photolibrary.com 5(TL);
Rex Features: David Cole Front Cover(BL), 1(BC), 5(B);
Courtesy of Visit Denmark.com: ©J. Buusman 30(TR).

All reasonable efforts have been made to ensure the reproduction of
content has been done with the consent of copyright owner.
If you are aware of any unintentional omissions, please contact the
publishers directly so that any necessary corrections may
be made for future editions.

Contents

Hej! – Hello!

We are the children of Denmark, and we can't
wait to share our lives with you in this book!

Welcome to Denmark!

We've got so much to show you! Let's start by telling you a little about our country. We hope you'll come and see Denmark for yourself some time soon!

NORWEGIAN SEA

SWEDEN

Malling

Hornsyld

DENMARK

Copenhagen

Bornholm

BALTIC SEA

GERMANY

POLAND

Our country

Denmark is in Northern Europe. It is part of an area known as Scandinavia, which also includes Norway, Sweden, and Iceland. Sea surrounds most of Denmark. Our country is made up of more than 400 islands as well as the mainland.

Our capital

Copenhagen is our capital city. The Queen of Denmark lives there. She is also Queen of Greenland and the Faroe Islands. Pictured here is the Danish Parliament building.

Land and climate

The land in Denmark is mostly low and flat. Inland, it is very green, and along the coasts there are huge sandy beaches. The climate is mild—winters are not too cold and summers are not too hot. It can be wet and windy, but the sea breeze is great for watersports!

Tourist spot

There are lots of exciting places to visit in Denmark. Legoland is one of the most famous—the Danes invented lego!

Our flag

Denmark's flag is the oldest national flag in the world.

National bird

Our national bird is the mute swan. We have lots of water birds and animals in Denmark.

Speak Danish!

hej—hello/hi

vi ses/farvel—goodbye

vær så venlig [vaer-so-venlie]—please

tak—thank you

5

Karina

Hi! My name is Karina Asmussen and I am 9 years old. I live with my mom, dad, and two big brothers in Hornsyld on the mainland of Denmark. My mischievous pet dog is called Tessi. She's almost two years old and she's very playful!

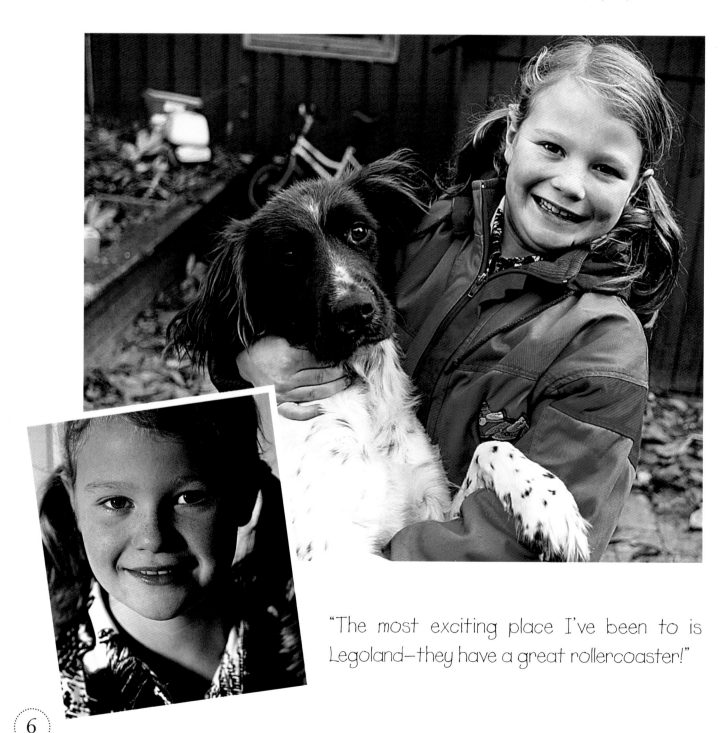

"The most exciting place I've been to is Legoland—they have a great rollercoaster!"

Here we are outside our house. My 20-year-old brother, Denni, is away right now. He's training to be a plumber. Next to me here is Daniel—he's 17 and he's a carpenter.

We have a chicken coop in the backyard—I like going out to collect the eggs.

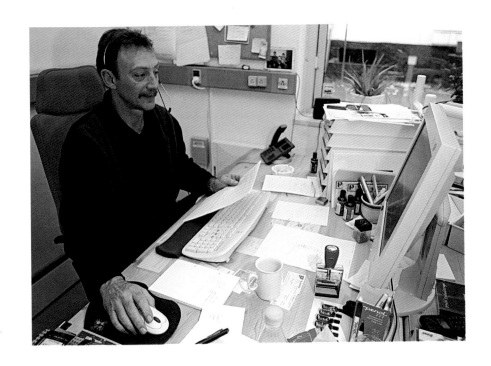

This is the office where Dad goes to work. He sells medicine on the internet. Mom works at home, looking after a group of small children.

Dad drives me to school on his way to work. We put my *bike* in the back of the car so I can bicycle home. School starts at 8:00 A.M.

My favorite lessons are art and music, because they're the most fun. Here I'm drawing a picture to illustrate the Bible story my teacher is reading.

There are 19 children in my class. At recess time I like playing this board game, called Kalaha, with some of the girls. I usually win!

We finish school at 11:30 A.M. on Mondays and 12:40 P.M. during the rest of the week. I say goodbye to my best friend, Laerke...

...and then I ride home! It's only a five-minute ride. I carry my books for homework in a rucksack on my back.

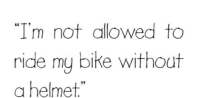

"I'm not allowed to ride my bike without a helmet."

9

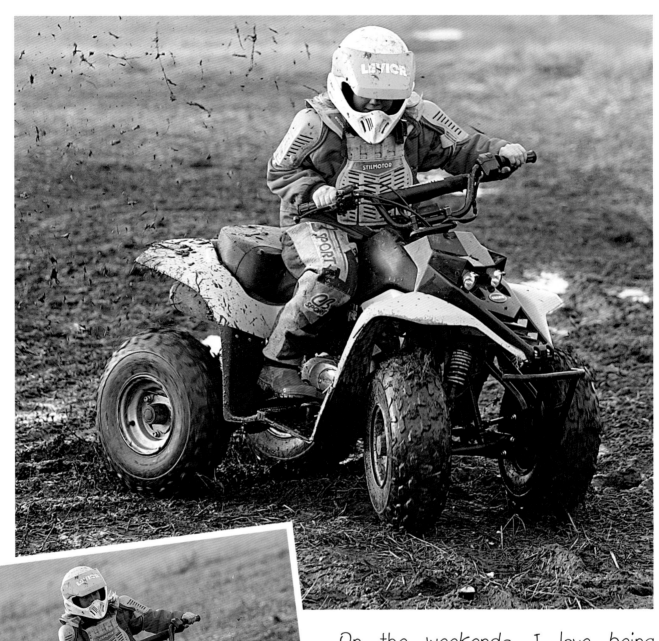

On the weekends, I love being outside, riding my motocross bike!

"My friends say I'm sweet, good, and tough!"

I also like running
around with Tessi...

...and making waffles for supper!

How I make waffles

I mix together some flour, baking
powder, sugar, and a pinch of salt.
I beat some milk, egg yolks, and
melted butter. Mom helps me cook
the batter on a hot waffle iron.

I have to be in bed by 9:30 P.M. In my room are some medals
I've won for playing soccer—another of my favorite hobbies!

11

Rasmus

Hello, I'm Rasmus Bille Brahe and I'm 7 years old. I live with my family on the island of Bornholm in the Baltic Sea. We moved here two years ago. It's quite a long way from the rest of Denmark, but we can get around by plane or ferry.

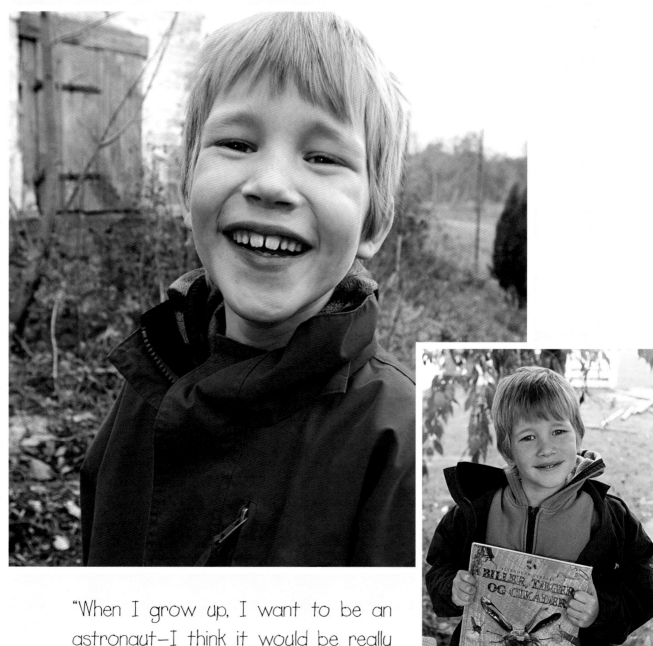

"When I grow up, I want to be an astronaut—I think it would be really funny to go into space!!"

This is my family! I have a sister, Sidse, who's 4 years old, and a baby brother named Johan. Mom is a teacher and Dad works here at home, designing websites.

We live on a farm, way out in the countryside. The mailman leaves our mail by the sign to our house, and we walk down to pick it up.

Here I am feeding Lille Miv, one of our pet cats— we have six cats altogether! We also have two dogs, a few chickens, some sheep, and a duck.

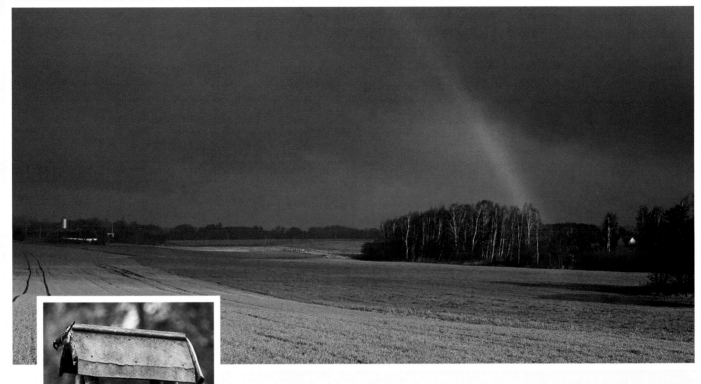

This is the view from our house—it's just been raining! On the land there is a forest, a stream, and a small lake. There are lots of little birds around—some of them come to feed on our bird table.

Farming country

Three-quarters of Denmark is covered in farmland. The main crops are cereals, like wheat and barley. Dairy farming is very common, too, so there is a lot of grass for grazing cows. Many people farm part-time, or as a hobby, and earn their living by doing other jobs.

I love it when Dad lets us ride on the trailer around the farm!

Our sheep have been grazing in the neighbors' field, so we're herding them back home.

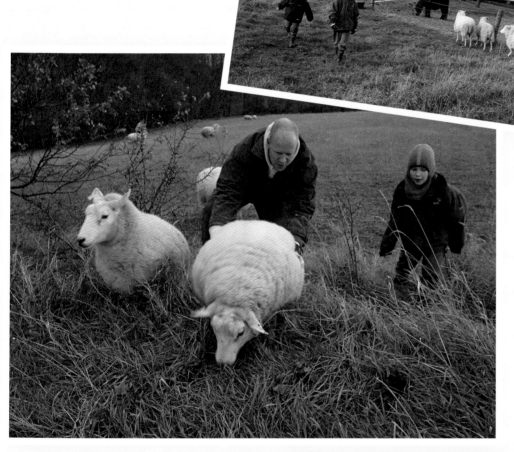

We return them safely, just as the light fades. In the winter here, it is dark by 3:00 or 4:00 P.M.!

Back inside, we have a big play fight—then we cuddle up on the sofa for a rest. I go to bed at 8:00 P.M., but I'm allowed to stay up later Fridays and Saturdays.

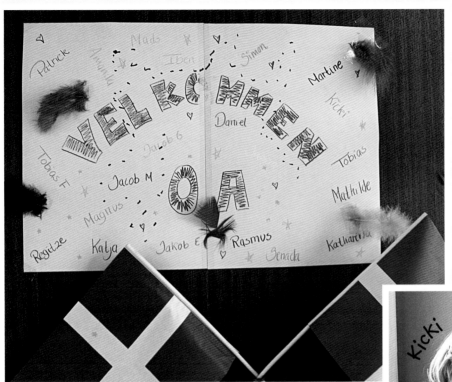

I go to school every morning from Monday to Friday. This is the sign on my classroom door—it says "Welcome," and all our names are written on it. I am in class OA.

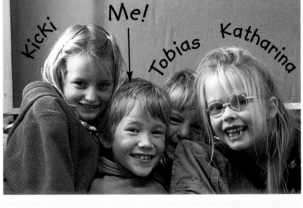

These are some of my classmates!

School years

Rasmus goes to pre-school, but he will soon move up to Grade 1. All children in Denmark have to go to school from the age of 7 until they are 16 (Grade 9). Pre-school and Grade 10 are optional. Lessons are in Danish, but everyone learns English from Grade 4 upward.

Friday is mostly play day. My best friend, Tobias, and I are excited because we've just won a game called Star of Africa!

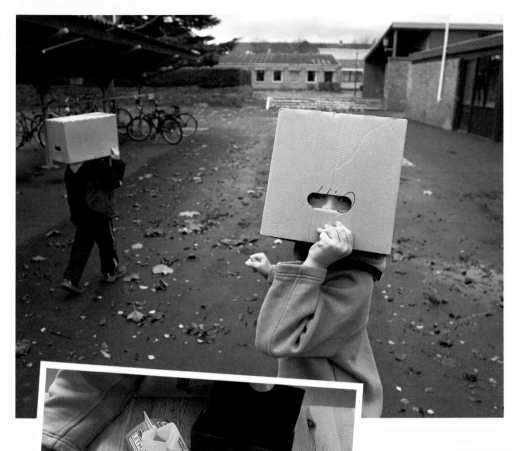

During recess, we go to get our milk and lunch packs. Tobias and I play games on the way!

Today's lunch is rye bread with ham and liver pâté, sausage in a roll, raw carrot, an apple, and cookies.

Black bread

Dark bread made from rye flour is very common in Denmark. It is often eaten as an open sandwich, called a "smørrebrød" [*smoerr-broeth*], with either ham, cheese, pâté, or fish.

At home my favorite foods are spare ribs and meatballs. I also love pancakes and homemade elderflower juice—we often have these when friends come for supper!

17

Millie and Sofia

Hej! We are Millie and Sofia Ramsgaard Skou—we are twins and we're 6 years old. Our Mom and Dad are divorced, but they both live in Copenhagen, so we have two great homes! In both places we share a room with a *bunk bed*.

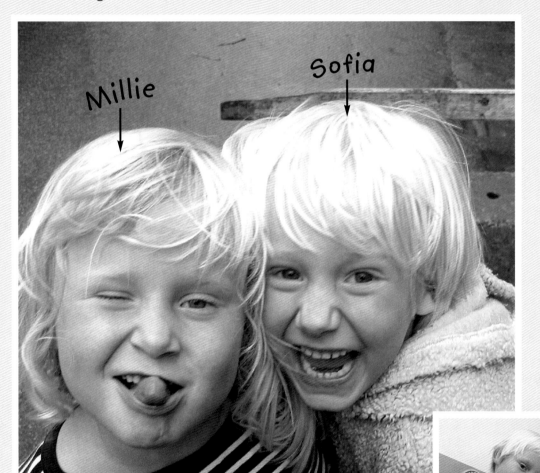

Millie

Sofia

"Our friends say we're really sweet. We get told off if we fight, scream, or stamp like elephants!"

Here we are eating dinner with Dad and his girlfriend, Kaisa. They have a baby named Olivia—our half sister.

This is us leaving for school with Mom (her name's Lisbeth) in the courtyard outside her building.

It's fun having a twin! We do lots of things together, like dancing to our favorite pop music...

Hans Christian Anderson

The famous author Hans Christian Anderson came from Denmark. He wrote hundreds of stories including *The Ugly Duckling, The Emperor's New Clothes,* and *The Little Mermaid.* He died in 1875, but the Danes still celebrate his birthday and his home is now a popular museum.

...reading Danish stories...

...and collecting Diddls! Diddls are the cute little characters on our cards and notepaper—we swap them with our friends. You can never have enough Diddls!

Every afternoon we go to after-school club. There are loads of activities. I love table soccer...

...and I like playing stores. We're selling a sticky cake made from sand and leaves—yum!

I made this bowl in the pottery room!

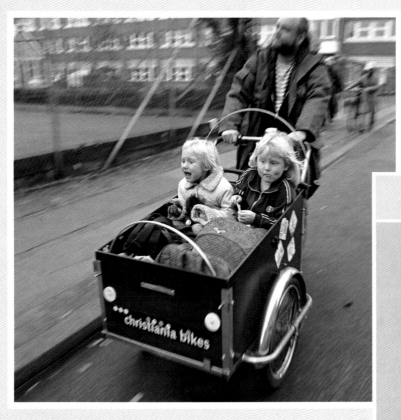

Sometimes we go shopping in town. Dad takes us in his bicycle cart—it's so exciting when he pedals fast!

Bicycling city

Lots of families in Copenhagen use bicycle carts for taking children to school or to the stores. Bicycling is the most popular way of getting around. You can even pay to borrow a bike from a stand, then get your money back when you return it.

The supermarket sells loads of fun things, including toys. We wish we could get more Diddls!

The money we spend in Denmark is called krone. Every week we each get 20 krone (almost $4) for pocket money.

Famous foods

Denmark has lots of pig farms, so pork is the most popular meat by far. People eat it roasted, in meatballs, in a wide variety of sausages, as hams, salami, and as bacon. Sweet, sticky Danish pastries (called "wienerbrød" *[viener-broeth]* in Denmark) are famous all over the world.

Today we're just shopping for food. I help to weigh the broccoli.

In the butcher shop, there are all kinds of delicious meats to choose from.

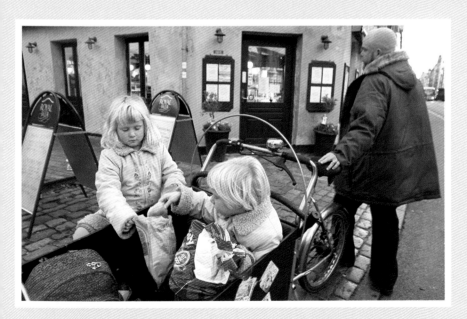

For a treat, we stop at the bakery to get some pastries and cakes!

"My favorite foods are Danish sausages and meatballs!" [Millie]

23

Nichlas

Hi, I'm Nichlas Nielsen Broch-Lips and I'm 9 years old. I live with my Mom, Dad, brother, and sister in Malling, on the eastern side of Denmark's mainland. We have two pet cats called Lakrids (meaning Licorice) and Killing (Kitten)!

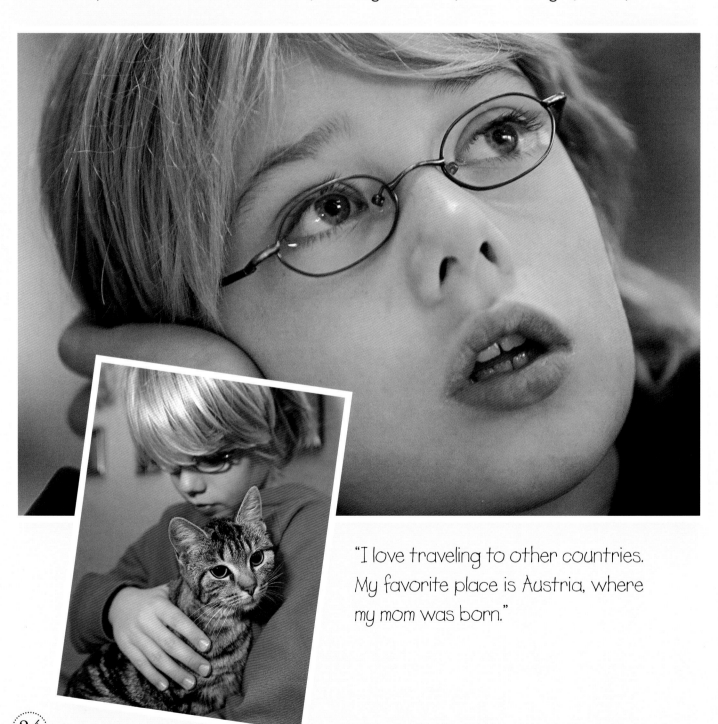

"I love traveling to other countries. My favorite place is Austria, where my mom was born."

Meet my family! My brother Mikkel is 6 years old and my sister Signe Ingrid is 3. Mom works in a shop that sells wooden toys and woolly clothes, and Dad is a social worker.

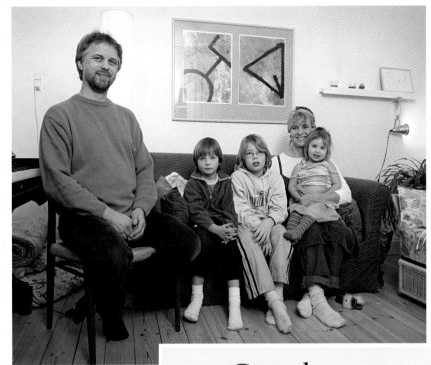

Cosy homes

Like the majority of people in Denmark, Nichlas's family have a comfortable home. Cosy times indoors with family and friends are an important part of Danish life—especially during the long, dark winters!

This is our house. The middle window on the top floor is my bedroom. In the backyard is an old water tower. A famous Danish comedian used to own it—and he made children's TV programs there!

My school is in Malling, not far away from our house. It takes me about 5 minutes to bicycle there. Lessons start at 8:15 A.M.—my favorite class is swimming, but I really like all my subjects!

"Our school is huge—there are 600 pupils and 45 teachers!"

Traveling around

People try not to use cars in Denmark, to avoid harming the environment. Like Nichlas, many children ride their bikes to school—most Danish people own a bike. There are also good bus and train services. Bridges join the different islands and there are ferry links, too.

These are two of my best friends, Søren and Aksel. We think we look cool in this picture!

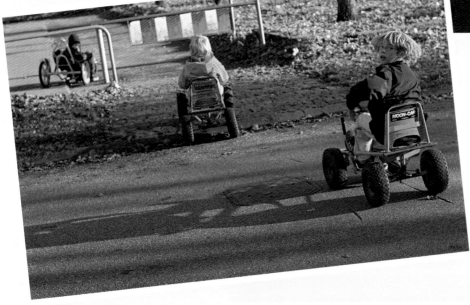

After school we go to the daycare center to play while our moms and dads are still at work. I love the Moon Cars!

When I get home, I have to do some homework. I'm pretty quick, so it usually takes me less than half an hour.

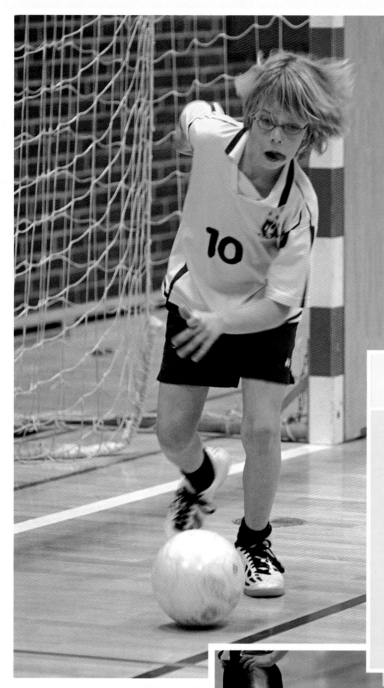

My favorite hobby is soccer. I'm a member of a local club called BMI. In the winter, I play indoors, once a week. In the summer, I play outside more often. I'm usually the goalkeeper.

Popular sports

Sports are very important in Denmark as a way of keeping fit, meeting new friends, and having fun. Football, badminton, swimming, and handball (like soccer, but played with the hand and a small ball) are all very popular. Because no one is far from the sea, lots of people also enjoy watersports, such as windsurfing and canoeing.

I do push-ups to help keep myself fit and strong!

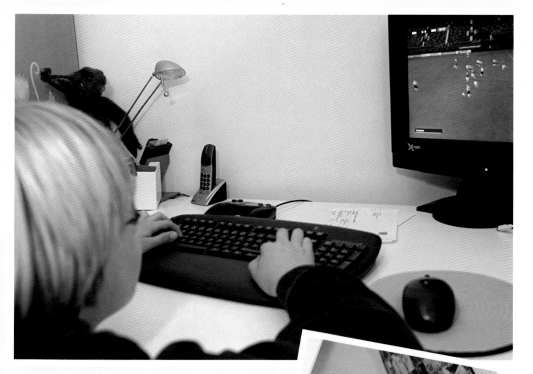

I also like playing soccer games on Mom and Dad's computer when they're not using it for work or writing emails!

On my bedroom wall I have soccer posters. I want to play for a professional team when I grow up. These are some of the medals I've won already.

My other hobby is drumming. I've been playing for two years and I'm crazy about it! We have a small studio at home where I can practice. I'm really into rock music—Linkin Park is my favorite band.

Our Year

Here are some important events in our calendar!

JANUARY

New Year's Day At the stroke of midnight, people welcome the new year with drinks and almond ring cakes.

FEBRUARY

Fastelavn Children dress up and go around local houses asking for treats. There is a game where we beat a big barrel with a stick until it breaks and candy falls out!

MARCH/APRIL

Nichlas's birthday: April 11th

Easter We have a special family meal and decorate the table with daffodils, yellow and purple napkins, and colored eggs. People give each other chocolate easter eggs.

Easter school vacation: March/April

Queen Margrethe's birthday We fly flags all around the country to congratulate the queen.

MAY

Great Prayer Day A national holiday when some people go to church and we traditionally eat hot wheat muffins.
Mother's Day We thank our moms for looking after us and give them cards and flowers.
Whitsun A religious festival and also the start of spring. We go outside with picnics and watch the sun dance in the sky!

JUNE

Constitution Day A national holiday when we all fly Danish flags.

Midsummer We light bonfires, have picnics, and sing songs.

JULY/AUGUST

Music festivals are held around the country, with all kinds of styles including jazz, rock, pop, and folk.

Karina's birthday: July 18th

Summer school vacation: July/August

SEPTEMBER

Rasmus's birthday: 17th September

Arhus festival The eastern city of Arhus hosts music and drama shows and also a Viking festival.

OCTOBER/NOVEMBER

There are film festivals in many parts of the country.

DECEMBER

Christmas Eve We fly flags and have a special evening meal with roast goose and Danish pastries.

Christmas school vacation: December/January

Millie & Sofia's birthday: December 2nd

Christmas Day We open the presents that are piled under our Christmas trees!

Vi ses! — Goodbye!

Glossary

cereals Grain crops such as wheat, barley, corn, and rye.

dairy farming Keeping cows to make use of their milk.

handball A game where goals are scored in a net like soccer, but players use their hands and a small ball.

kalaha A board game that's popular in Scandinavia. It is based on an old African game played with pebbles on a pitted wooden board.

rye bread A dark, heavy bread made from rye flour instead of wheat flour.

Scandinavia A region in Northern Europe that usually includes Denmark, Norway, Sweden, and Iceland. Finland is sometimes considered part of Scandinavia, too.

smørrebrød A Danish open sandwich made from rye bread with various toppings.

Index